# A Child's Missal
## The Eucharist

*A Visual Prayerbook Of The Paschal Mystery*

PATMOS
TOOLS FOR WORSHIP

*"Do This In Memory Of Me"*
(Luke 22:19)

# How to Use This Book

When we attend Mass we enter a world that is partly visible and partly invisible. A world of symbols and rituals, through which we remember Christ's saving deeds and renew his Sacrifice. It is a world so full of meaning that even the holiest and wisest never stop wondering at its mystery.

So how do we begin to understand the mystery of the Mass? How do we begin to understand what's going on around us as we sit, kneel, or stand in the presence of the Heavenly court?

St. Paul tells us that through visible things we come to understand things that are invisible. So we watch the actions of the priest, listen to the music, smell the incense as it rises with our prayers to God. And these become not only the way we pray but also the symbols through which we understand our own prayer—and what God has done for us.

This Child's Missal is meant to help you in the same way. It uses pictures and artwork to express the mysteries of the Mass. It is like a window through which you can see the invisible world that takes place around you.

Use this Missal to pray at Mass. But also use it to learn about the Mass at home or in catechism class. Parents will also learn as they teach their children through this visual prayerbook.

On the following page you will find a guide that will help you understand more about how to learn and pray with this Child's Missal.

Christ's entire life was liturgical. See how the scenes of his life relate to each moment of the Mass.

Explore each art piece to glean from it many stories and symbolic meanings, like how the wedding feast at Cana foreshadowed Christ's changing wine into his own blood at Mass.

Sacred Scripture gives understanding and prepares your heart for God.

The Low Mass has all the essential elements of a High Mass, though it expresses them in a less solemn way. In the corner you will find a soft engraving of the corresponding Low Mass scene.

Names too are rich with meaning. Think about why each part of the Mass has the name that it is given. (Note that the name on the left is in Latin.)

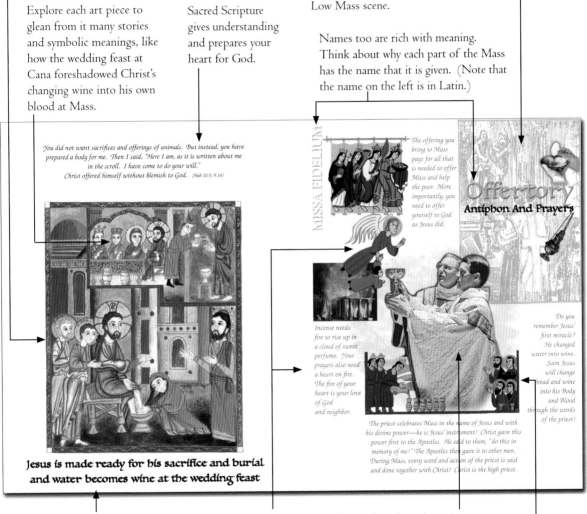

*You did not want sacrifices and offerings of animals. But instead, you have prepared a body for me. Then I said, "Here I am, as it is written about me in the scroll. I have come to do your will." Christ offered himself without blemish to God.* (Heb 10:5; 9:14)

MISSA FIDELIUM

*The offering you bring to Mass pays for all that is needed to offer Mass and help the poor. More importantly, you need to offer yourself to God as Jesus did.*

Offertory
Antiphon And Prayers

*Incense needs fire to rise up in a cloud of sweet perfume. Your prayers also need a heart on fire. The fire of your heart is your love of God and neighbor.*

*Do you remember Jesus' first miracle? He changed water into wine. Soon Jesus will change bread and wine into his Body and Blood through the words of the priest!*

*The priest celebrates Mass in the name of Jesus and with his divine power—he is Jesus' instrument! Christ gave this power first to the Apostles. He said to them, "do this in memory of me!" The Apostles then gave it to other men. During Mass, every word and action of the priest is said and done together with Christ! Christ is the high priest.*

**Jesus is made ready for his sacrifice and burial and water becomes wine at the wedding feast**

Each part of the Mass has an overall theme. Everything else can be thought of in relation to this theme.

The Guardian Angel guides the boy Adam in his understanding and prayerful attention at Mass. Meditate on his words and follow his advice! He speaks to you too in the light colored text.

Think about how the main action of the Mass relates to the art that surrounds it, especially the picture on the far left side of the page.

"A picture paints a thousand words". Try to read the meaning of the mystery as it appears in the surrounding artwork.

# Jesus enters triumphantly into Jerusalem to offer the sacrifice of his paschal mystery

# Introit Antiphon
## Entrance Procession

Mass begins when the priest enters your chapel, just as Jesus entered Jerusalem before his sacrifice on the cross.

Ask God to forgive your sins by singing the Kyrie. Then sing the Gloria, a hymn to thank God for bringing peace to earth by the sacrifice of the Mass.

Sing to welcome Jesus coming in the priest!

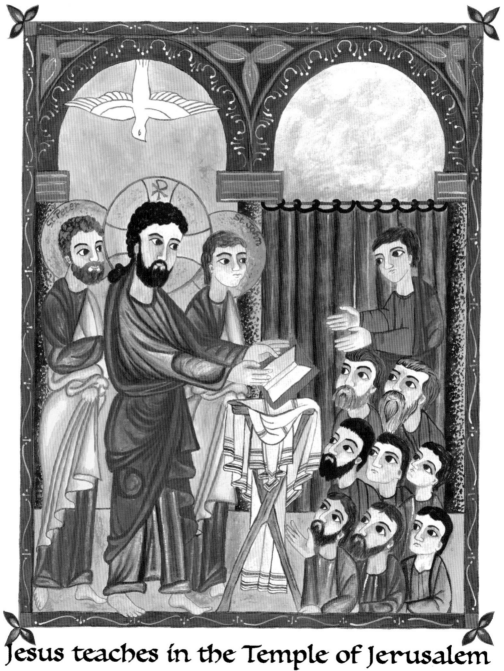

Jesus teaches in the Temple of Jerusalem
preparing the people for his sacrifice

## LITURGIA VERBI

Mass began with you praying to God. Now it is God's turn to speak to you. He feeds your heart with his words and teachings. He shows you the path to follow: Jesus is the way, the truth, and the life.

# Readings
## And Sermon

The Church teaches you like your mother. The Bible and the priest tell you the story of Jesus and the fathers of our faith. The Church uses music and teaches you to sing your prayers. Do you see the chapel's beautiful pictures and statues? This is how the Church teaches you to give glory to God.

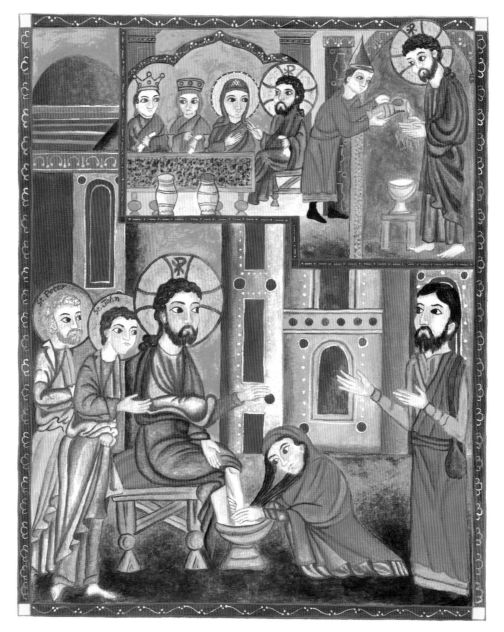

# Jesus is made ready for his sacrifice and burial and water becomes wine at the wedding feast

The offering you bring to Mass pays for all that is needed to offer Mass and help the poor. More importantly, you need to offer yourself to God as Jesus did.

# Offertory
## Antiphon And Prayers

Incense needs fire to rise up in a cloud of sweet perfume. Your prayers also need a heart on fire. The fire of your heart is your love of God and neighbor.

Do you remember Jesus' first miracle? He changed water into wine. Soon Jesus will change bread and wine into his Body and Blood through the words of the priest!

The priest celebrates Mass in the name of Jesus and with his divine power—he is Jesus' instrument! Christ gave this power first to the Apostles. He said to them, "do this in memory of me!" The Apostles then gave it to other men. During Mass, every word and action of the priest is said and done together with Christ! Christ is the high priest.

Jesus loved his disciples to the end. And now he showed them how much he really loved them. When the hour came, Jesus and his apostles were at supper. Then Jesus lifted his eyes to heaven and prayed: "Father, I have glorified you on earth. I have finished the work you gave me to do. So now glorify me with the glory I had with you before the world began." *(Jn 13:1; Lk 22:14; Jn 17:1,4)*

# Jesus sings a hymn of thanksgiving for God's work of Creation and Redemption

Are you ready to sing with the angels? Thank God for his greatest gift. This gift is the work that Jesus did. He created us. He rescued us from the devil's power. And he made us a holy people.

Sing with the angels: Sanctus! Sanctus! Sanctus!

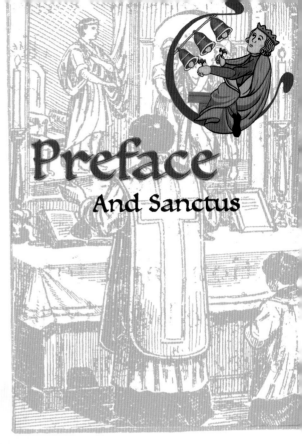

# Preface
## And Sanctus

The preface of the Mass is like the preface to a book. It tells you what you are expected to do, and why you should to do it. It also shows you that the angels are joining you in what you are doing.

When you pray you "lift up your mind and heart to God." You need to pay close attention. The center and most important part of the Mass now begins. You should not be distracted!

*When Jesus had finished praying, he left with his disciples and went across the Kidron Valley. On the other side was a garden, and they went into it. Jesus said to them, "My soul is very sorrowful, even unto death. Stay here and keep watch with me."* (Jn 18:1; Mt 26:38)

# Jesus prays for all in the Garden of Olives and asks for our prayers

# Intercession
## For The Living

A single Mass can help every person on earth. Join your prayers to those of Jesus. Pray for all the people you know. Pray also for all those you do not know.

The Apostles fell asleep when Jesus was praying before his sacrifice. This is your chance to do better. Console the suffering Jesus!

Besides prayers, offer your help to someone in need after Mass. You need to love not just with words. You need to put your love into practice!

*"The Father loves me because I give up my life. No one takes it from me. I give it up myself."* (Jn 10:17)

Christ came as the high priest. He entered the Most Holy Sanctuary by shedding his own blood. And he has freed us from sin forever. (Heb 9:11, 12)

# Jesus offers himself willingly as a victim for the expiation of our sins

The old Jewish priests offered lambs for people's sins. They did this to show how Jesus was going to come later and truly be the Lamb of God who takes away the sins of the world. Covering the head of the lamb meant that sin was now placed on it.

# Oblation
## Offering And Epiclesis

It was not easy for Jesus to offer himself like a meek lamb. But he was very willing to do it for the love of you. He knew that God wanted him to be a sin offering.

The sacrifice of Jesus is also your sacrifice. Join your pains to the suffering of Jesus. Now ask God to sanctify your gift. Also ask him to make of you an eternal oblation.

Notice how the priest covers the bread and wine with his hands. This is just like what the Old Testament priests did. Now your sins are placed on Jesus. He died that you may live a new life of holiness with God.

*I received from the Lord what I pass on to you. On the night he was betrayed, he took bread. And when he had given thanks, he broke it. He said, "This is my body, which is given for you. Do this in memory of me." In the same way, after supper he took the cup and said, "This cup is the new covenant in my blood. Whenever you drink it, do it in memory of me."* (1 Cor 11:23-24)

# Jesus dies on the cross for us as his Body and Blood separate

# Consecration
## Of The Body And Blood

The sacrifice of Calvary happened once. It cannot happen again. Nor can it be repeated. The ritual action of the priest makes present again the same sacrifice of Good Friday. This is the way you can join in!

The old sacrifices of the Jews had some power to forgive sins. But how much more the Body and Blood of Jesus! This power is infinite, for this is the sacrifice of a man who is also God.

"My Lord and My God!"

Your eyes see only the actions of the priest. Your faith sees the miracle that takes place. St. Anthony once showed the Eucharist to a hungry mule. Instead of eating his oats, the mule adored Jesus!

*We believe in God who raised Jesus our Lord from the dead. Jesus was handed over to die because of our sins. He was raised to life to make us right with God. Now we have peace with God because of our Lord Jesus Christ. Let us be joyful because we hope to share in God's glory.* (Rom 4:24-25; 5:2)

# Jesus rises and ascends to heaven after his sacrifice and death

We pray with Jesus to the Father. We offer the sacrifice. It is the sacrifice of Jesus. It must also be your sacrifice: your life, your will. You are one with Christ. What you offer as a member of the Church is offered to God in Christ!

# Memorial
## Passion, Resurrection & Ascension

What a joy to know that Jesus is preparing a place for you in heaven!

You should not just watch the Mass. You must join with the priest and offer again all Jesus did for you: his death on the Cross, his rising from the tomb, and his going back to heaven.

We don't just remember Jesus with our minds. At the consecration, his passion, resurrection and ascension become truly present. But we can see this only with the eyes of faith.

*Christ really was raised from the dead. He is the first of all those who will rise. A man brought death into the world. And a man brought the resurrection of the dead. Because of Adam, all people die. Because of Christ, all will be brought to life.* (1 Cor 15:20-22)

# Jesus raises his friend Lazarus
# and frees the dead by the power of his sacrifice

The Mass allows the angels to bring newly-washed souls up to heaven. They live there with God and all the saints.

# Remembrance
## Of The Dead

Now pray for those who are "resting in the sleep of peace" but cannot yet be fully with God. Their sins are washed away in the blood of the Lamb. The Mass presents again that Blood to purify us all.

# Jesus comes back in the clouds of heaven to reign over all peoples in holiness

This is a beautiful moment. Jesus is at the center of the whole universe. He brings all creatures back to God and comes down in glory to reign with us.

# Canon's End
## And Minor Elevation

The priest offers the sacrifice to the Trinity by lifting the chalice and host together. This is called the minor elevation.

PER IPSUM ET CUM IPSO ET IN IPSO

Jesus reigns in the Church and will come back one day just as he left: riding victorious on the clouds of heaven!

The Father asked Jesus to rescue you from the devil. He also asked him to pay for your sins. Jesus did it by his death and by his resurrection. The Mass re-presents both in the consecration. This gives perfect honor and glory to God the Father in the unity of the Holy Spirit.

*The kingdom of heaven is like a king who prepared a wedding feast for his son. He sent his servants out into the streets. They gathered everyone they could find, both good and bad. Soon the wedding hall was filled with guests.* (Mt 22:2, 10)

# Jesus teaches the disciples how to pray:
# "Our Father, who art in heaven!"

# Preparation
## For Communion

Communion is a part of Jesus' sacrifice. First came the offering of his life. At the center was the laying down of his life. Now comes the sharing of his life.

You became a child of God at Baptism. You also learned the laws of God from the Church. Now you can truly talk to your heavenly Father. Use the prayer that Jesus taught us: "Our Father..." By Jesus' sacrifice, you are truly a son of God. It's not just a name. It's a reality!

The food you are about to receive is Jesus' Body broken on the cross. It is also his Blood shed upon the cross. But it is also his Body and Blood re-united in the living, glorified Christ after the Resurrection. He is truly the lamb of God. He was sacrificed for our sins. He is now going to be your food.

*"I am the bread of life. Your ancestors ate manna in the desert, but they died. I am the living bread that came down from heaven. Anyone who eats this bread will live forever. The bread I will give is my body. I will give it for the life of the world."* (Jn 6:48-51)

# Jesus gives his Body and Blood as Moses gave the Hebrews manna

# Communion

## And Thanksgiving

Receive Jesus in Communion like the Apostles did during the Last Supper.

The altar and the re-presentation of Jesus' sacrifice are the center of Christian life. The life of God flows from the altar to all the Church. It comes to you in Holy Communion. It stays afterwards in the Real Presence of Jesus in the Eucharist.

Your Guardian Angel is here to help you receive Jesus into your heart.

The angels brought food to Moses and the Jews. This food made them strong to travel to the Promised Land. Holy Communion is now your daily spiritual food. It will give you eternal life. It will give you the life of God. It will make you strong to travel from this earth to heaven. And it will unite you with all other members of Jesus' Mystical Body.

*"All authority in heaven and on earth has been given to me. Therefore, go and make disciples of all nations. Baptize them in the name of the Father and of the Son and of the Holy Spirit. Teach them to obey everything I have commanded you. I am with you always, even to the end of time."* (Mt 28:18-20)

# Jesus blesses and sends his disciples to preach the Gospel to the whole world

ITE MISSA EST

# Final Blessing
## And Last Gospel

The word "Mass" comes from the Latin word for the official dismissal of the people.

The Mass is now finished. You are blessed by the priest. A blessing gives you the life-giving force of God to be strong in your Christian life.

Stay a few minutes to thank God for the Mass.

Jesus loves all people. He sent the Apostles to preach the truth to the whole world. They worked hard "to catch" souls in the boat of the Church. Thanks to them you are now a Christian! You also need to go out into the deep of the world to fish souls for Jesus.

# About the Artists

Sister Anna Marie McCormick is a self-taught artist from San Jose, California. She began her painting career as a toddler with finger paints and never looked back. Number eight of nine children, Sister Anna Marie credits her parents for giving her the creative inspiration. Sister Anna Marie has been published for her work with silhouette paper cuts of the Blessed Virgin and her icons of the Mysteries of the Rosary.

A self-taught artist from Morristown, New Jersey, Mr. Adam Repka has been painting ever since he can remember. Adam has devoted his artistic talent to decorative art, something for which he has received a fair bit of notoriety in the eastern U.S. This Child's Missal marks the first of Adam's published work. While Adam very much enjoys making chairs, tables, and entire homes into works of art, he looks forward to applying his talents to more printed work in the future.

*Sister Anna Marie is responsible for painting all the scenes on the left-side page of this book, while Adam Repka created the illustrations on the right-side pages. Below are examples of the approach each of these artists has taken with this book.*

*Original 8th century artwork*

Sr. Anna Marie took 8th century icons (shown on the left) and transformed them into a more child-friendly style (shown below). She also added elements to enrich them theologically. In this example, she

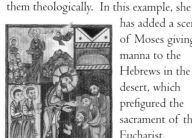

has added a scene of Moses giving manna to the Hebrews in the desert, which prefigured the sacrament of the Eucharist.

Adam's work also involved reinterpreting ancient Christian icons for a contemporary youthful audience. Below is an example of an ancient painting of the miracle at Cana followed by Adam's rendition of the same scene. Adam's

angel and little boy were inspired by a Medieval depiction of Dante being guided by Beatrice through Paradise (in the *Divine Comedy*).